CU0915098836

# THE INVISIBLE

# THE INVISIBLE

ALESSIO ZANELLI

Greenwich Exchange
London

Greenwich Exchange, London
First published in Great Britain in 2024
All rights reserved

Printed and bound by imprintdigital.com
Cover design by December Publications
Tel: 07951511275

Author website: www.alessiozanelli.it

Greenwich Exchange website: www.greenex.co.uk

Cataloguing in Publication Data is available from the British Library

ISBN: 978-1-910996-71-3

To my parents

*We are more closely connected to the invisible than to the visible.*

—Novalis

# CONTENTS

# TRANSITION HENDECAPOEM

*Transition End*

Pensive, on the cusp. A place to be alone.
In bad company, though. No one believes it's
the time, or scans the blue. All just scream and toss
like mad. They don't know why but feel impelled to
scramble down. It is no common height. They can
find no path away, giddiness numbs their brains
and melts their legs. Is this chastisement? I'll have
to confront the upheaval pressed by throngs of
clueless loons. No more times of day, one endless
sunset. Impatient, edgy, yet home and dry.
Could what I'm watching be already sunrise?

\*

*Onset*

None of the survivors remembers. It must
have been cold, sunny with a uniform snow
cover and a high albedo. Or else my
unconditional love for the White Lady
would be hard to explain. I delivered my
first cry in a delivery room of a
maternity hospital managed by nuns,
nowadays a luxury old people's home.
I can only imagine Mom's joy, beyond
words despite the long pains and the C-section,
until her eyes alighted on my right foot.

\*

*Verdicts*

To elect the left as my takeoff leg came
naturally, the very moment I stopped
crawling on all fours. It was certainly not
such a minor anomaly to blame for
my sporting failures. Ballgames never were my
forte, teams annoyed me. I was a loner,
but for the rest a defiant kid like most.
Luminaries had expressed discordant views.
In the end my parents, haunted with doubts, did
not give full credit to either. Lucky me.
Decades later roads would pass final verdicts.

*

*Rhaetia*

The time came to put head and legs to the test,
challenge the giants looming in the distance.
The manifold infinities could wait. It
took Tiberius and Drusus less than a
year to make it a province. I find treasures
to this day, as I walk through the steep defile
to the brink between two worlds. Down one side a
tear will swell the Danube, down the other one
the Po. At the foot of awe-inspiring walls,
above the smugglers' track, gentians try man's trust.
Those slopes and crests have branded me deep inside.

*

*Mesozoic*

To call them heroes may be regarded as
an overstatement, but that's precisely what
they are to me. Back when I used to ramble
from bad to worse, incapable of telling
Cerces from Calypsos, they often banged me
out of trouble with their mighty roar. Eras
have been kind to them. After over half a
century, the dinosaurs' merry-go-round
is still revolving freely, to the delight
of most ultramodern, sophisticated,
mammal-like parasites who'd want them extinct.

*

*Iliad*

Get it together. Tidy yourself up. Put
on a winning smile. Make a nimble approach.
Don't look awkward or stilted. Break the ice. Try
not to stutter or clutter. Avoid clichés.
Use pauses. Go easy on wittiness, a
bit of banter is fine, too much is baleful.
Wait for a reply. How many times did I
revise this hendecalogue? Probably not
enough. Why has it always been as tough as
laying siege to a city? I thought I was
Odysseus, but I was Agamemnon.

*

*Odyssey*

Ithaca does not exist. It must remain
a fancy, dragging us on, from league to league,
alert to reefs, shallows, tempests, mermaids. An
eternal token of all that we pursue,
which shifts away as we draw near. Tenebrous
landfalls, I've sighted many. Some I've shunned, and
some I've rushed into. I never ran across
Tiresias, and if I had, I wouldn't
have inquired about my future. Neither faith
nor fate. Dreams, at last, have made me plot my course.
We're through what we're through to be right where we are.

\*

*Pheidippides*

They say you never forget your first. True. I
tend to forget all the others, except the
last. The roads you run on, the towns you traverse
and the hills you ascend, they all have no name.
The final destination is always the
same. And to think I started it almost as
a joke. I didn't plan on such a mileage,
nor did I imagine it was my bag. I
don't bring good news. Before, I didn't know where
the coastal plain of Marathon was, nor had
I ever heard about hemerodromi.

\*

*Homes*

The old roundabout had long been my passion.
I wished to pay a visit to the real
place, where it had spun from. I've paid quite a few.
I've seen the circles, the squares, the dales, the moors.
Now I know what I've seen is a second home.
And not too far from home, what a twist of fate,
one day I found a gorgeous piece of it, as
if waiting for me. My missing half, which I
was looking for, and which had left home in turn
a fifth of a lifetime before. Twin loves and
twin firesides, that's what Albion means to me.

\*

*Farewell*

The rushes to the hospital seemed like a
distant memory. Commuting between home
and the OAT lab was the new routine.
The sea was calm again, even too flat. No
one suspected the weather change underway.
Clouds had been gathering unseen beyond the
horizon. A vast disturbance, no normal
storm, which soon occluded the sky. To its depths.
Acclimatized to downpours, then regular
rain, at last soft drizzle, utter stillness took
us by surprise. Till we had to let her go.

\*

*Transition Start*

I go visit the precinct at random, now
and again, driven by instinct. If there are
people, I normally don't enter. I like
it deserted, at the close of day. It makes
me hyperreactive, expands my mind, but
only if I stay amid the yard. A while.
Those walls of grave plaques cause me catalepsy.
I could do nothing there for more than a few
minutes. To transit the abode's heritage,
reach past and rise up, I must be quick, then walk
away. Each time return a perfect stranger.

# THE BRIGAND

I only wished to start a new one.

May this be home? Millstone grit and heather?
Undulating pastures and drystack fences?
The dales once ruled by the Brigantes?
A place this ancient—where days glide by so slow
and human presence is not a fundamental trait—
surely wrings my deepest strings.
Lost in it, on my own, carrying nothing,
and nothing loaded on my mind—
it looks, sounds and smells
like I had always been part of it.
Everything fits just right, and I feel good.
Like I had been treading these moors
and my thoughts ascending these ridges—
to see what runs away beyond the hilltops—
since the very moment I was born.
Still, it is when the light abates
and cloudbanks slither down to cloak the slopes—
emulating lowland fog—
when the lines of trees fade on the horizon
and silence appropriates each quiver of life—
coming to nestle in the most distant memories—
that I do find myself at home.
But sooner or later the sun—as precious as gold
and of such rare beauty on this drowsy, sullen land,
orchestrator of grandiose skies—
reminds me who I am, or who at least I used to be,
where my roaming soul indeed belongs,
hurling me a thousand miles southeast.
For I am a brigand here—
my loot the eternal swish of branches in the westerlies
and the instancy of desperate sunsets over the crests.

A sly usurper, a thief of space and time.
All while galaxies out there keep on drifting,
and the clock cannot be zeroed.

I only wished to start a new one.

## DEAR OLD BELOVED PADAN FOG

*Fümàna* (fʊe-mä-nä seems to be its best possible
English transcription, with the stress on the second syllable)
is the dialect word by which they call the fog where I live.
From *föm* (fəm), *fumo* in Italian, meaning smoke (but also fume).
The Po Plain wouldn't exist without it.
In the old days it used to be a constant—in wintertime—
and often showed as early as October or as late as April.
And it could be really dense, surly, virtually impenetrable,
but never really nasty. Only people acting foolishly
could render it wicked dangerous, even lethal.
Nowadays youth can barely recognize the likes of it.

My blood and nerves feel like missing it sometimes,
as if regretting its equalizing power, its discreet ubiquity.
Among all meteors, it's the only one sort of sentient,
I would dare say, the most politically correct.
I surely miss it now—I haven't got a clue why—
while sipping a Czech pilsner, sunk in a cushioned armchair,
an American poet's book open on my lap, in a silent conservatory.
Tired from a long hike, squinting at an unusually clear Yorkshire sky,
waiting for the heather to blossom over the moors up the hills.
A slightly staid, perfunctory sneer pictured on my face.
The mind on an errand a thousand miles away via the smartphone.

## HAVING BEING

A summit is mirrored
in a small lake
in a dell.

Never have I
crossed the dell,
swum the small lake,
ascended the summit,
but I've been watching
or else imagining them
for quite a long time,
happy they are there.

A dell
with a small lake
surmounted by a summit,
my very self watching
or else imagining them.

## NATIVE PLACE

*La chiesetta là in collina*
*legge al mondo il suo destin.*
—Pino Ruggeri


The unease it may elicit
from those who searched
into the name—only a few do
know it comes from "morbid"—
appears disproportionate to such
a nothing of a creek I'm old enough
to have had the chance to bathe in, a
young lad so scared of streaming water.

The belfry, jutting from the hillock, lures
the visitors from afar—looking higher
than it is—a harmless trick devised
by what once was a teeny clot of
houses, today an aging village
that's long lost its pristine
innocence and is vainly
reclaiming its soul.

# ONE LAST GIN AND TONIC AT LA HACIENDA

*Another G&T please,*
*with some orange peel.*
You try to drown
your ailing thoughts,
they seem to sink at first,
but in the end resurface,
can stay afloat on any booze.
You stay sick in turn.
Luckily for me,
there are cool bartenders,
quick and gentle youths.
They are smart,
besides professional,
can read both your face and mind,
have good words and smiles for you,
with discretion,
but know when to become serious,
wearing a mildly reproving look
over their indulgent grin,
and definitely convince you
that the time has come,
however bad it all still feels,
to put down the Copa de Balon
and walk back home.

## NOWHEREVERYWHERE

There is nobody of whom to ask directions,
no way at all to get to know my whereabouts.
You may go searching for years, or never move:
your chance of locating me would hardly increase,
even if you swept the whole of space from star to star.

Because I'm here, and there, and everywhere:
I'm over this plain and on top of Everest,
by this river and on Lake Baikal shore,
on this street and in Times Square,
in this town and thro' Beijing.

Yes I'm in Rome and in Singapore,
in Buenos Aires and in Antananarivo,
in Moscow, in Wellington and in Tokyo;
in, or far from, every given city of the Earth.
Along the Equator and amid Antarctica at once.

I'm in deserts, in swamps, in glaciers and in oceans;
I'm in billabongs, in maelstroms and in geysers;
I'm also in the mist and in the highest clouds.
I may be right here, or who knows where:
nowhere, or where the universe ends.

## A TRIAD OF VISIONS

It doesn't fear the excess of heat,
a flower bloomed too soon
deceived by the sun.
It fears the cold, and the wind,
and unsought solitude.
It fears to go limp unpicked.

A scratchless child,
I saw a bolide
blazing through the dark.
I followed its trail across nowhere,
only to find myself exactly where I'd left,
a branded man.

Back in the folds of time,
at the core of the African cradle,
hominids rose and challenged a world
ruled by absentee gods.
Their progeny strives against the vacuum
nature is paving the way to.

## THE ROAD AND I

I used to spend my days
along its fluid lines,
whatever end they led me to,
to take it by the length,
no matter what the sky looked like,
to straighten it by its bends
and stretch it by its ups and downs,
though just on my mind.
The asphalt was my friend,
and also earth and gravel were,
so that I only rarely felt alone.
I never expected a real conversation
but always hoped for some chat
from time to time,
and now that I've lost count
of how many miles,
silence is the very reason
I'm still running for.
Deeper than it ever was.
I can shout at myself
without uttering a sound,
or swear aloud at the horizon
making fun of me,
even curse the surface I tread.
Absolutely sure the road will not talk back.

# THE SEEKERS OF BODIES

Who goes for me?
Who asks my name?

Perhaps the ones I still haven't loved?
I've always ignored?
I've never looked in the eye?

There is no hope for them,
no particular regard
and no special mention.
I barely know they exist.

They're after me though,
I feel them breathing down my neck.
Their gazes scan me from tip to toe
as if I were their only reason for living.

They don't know that what they see
is mere illusion,
my shadow materialized,
made into a slippery body.
And it deceives without restraint.

The soul languishes thousands of miles away,
in the wasteland where I left it against the shadow.
No trace of the true body,
and they who seek it,
they've got the void painted on the face.

# LACH DI CIÀZ

Foot after foot
the peaks emerge
from the forest.

My ghost awakes
and rises up,
above the trees,
above the crest
of aging dreams.

My eyes command
what used to rule
my head below,
but not the heights,
the upper heights
of yore of which
I must let go.

Let go to go.

## VIEW

Over the mountains, the horizon along the crests.
Not a sound all around. Conifers in the shade of twilight,
then snowfields, tongues and cirques of glaciers, walls of rock.
The joint line of sky and earth like a boundary between selves.
Below, the call of home, at the bottom of the valley,
a walk through the dark of the night in the light of the soul.
But not before a glimpse at the flight in circles of the eagle,
under a moon slice, an embroidery against the heavens.
More than enough for today, quite a portion of everything
on view above out there as well as deep down inside.

# TIME

They were right. We would get to know the hoax.
They had ridden the carousel before.
The swallows have always been returning,
only fewer with every passing year,
though they have never really gone away.
Now they speak to me in dreams, one by one.
The time has come. To regret time. And all.
We are drops off the stalactites of time,
settling the concretions of memory.
And the sun burns on. Up and down around.

## THE RUNNER

On feet of dreams the runner's headed to land's end.
She knows the horizon keeps receding while she's running,
but she runs as though it didn't.
A finish line is not her aim.
Along the pathway time's not measured in seconds but in paces,
in fact a runner's time and space commingle.
The run will come to a stop where dreams dissolve,
and dreams don't hinge on time or space
but on the run itself.
Land's end is but a moving sight, the pathway a circle.

## A WALK AT DUSK

Some say the twilight's best
enjoyed by rocking on
the porch. Until it's dark.
I think it is no time
to rest. Its hues can be
much brighter than the day's.
Then who recalls the dawn's?
I'm going to shake off
the blues, put on my shoes,
step out towards the west
and meet the setting sun.
I'm in no rush, and yet
I have to mind each pace.
The dusk, you know, that's earned.

## THE STREAM

They go. Normally in dribs and drabs,
at times in a row. However, they go.
For a while I follow them with my eyes,
as soon as they show up on the road,
as long as they keep within the horizon.
And when at last they're lost to sight,
I'm still able to hear them whisper away.
I discern where each one comes from,
make out the path behind, assess the gait,
yet I've no clue about where they head.
One day I'll join the stream, and I sure will.

# CIRCLER

At last you cannot but slow down,
although the tyrant's speeding up.
Footprints fall over into footprints,
stillness broadens around,
solitude deepens in.

Much more void than anyone can use,
not enough the light against the night.
You tread a furrow on your circle path,
while days connect the dots
as the crow flies.

## THE CART PUSHER

They are taking forests down,
digging the bowels of the earth,
moving the course of rivers,
strewing debris in the exosphere,
littering all that can be littered.
They think it is their right to do so,
and there is no one else's right,
neither present nor future.
I keep walking my own path by night,
as insignificant as a speck of dust,
pushing my little cart along,
only stopping every now and then
to pick bits of land for my collection,
watching the sky all the time
to check if the moon is still there.
Feeling as guilty as them.

# FROM SCRATCH

*The Planets* play, greet another day,
another year, just afoot in the drizzle.
The freeze has gone, a deceiving pawn,
all those who shudder call out for more.
Entangled in the strings, without wings,
the only escape is to look back a while.
Not too long though, or too long ago,
what can still be changed looms ahead.
All there is to know goes with the snow,
no one has business exploring the beyond.
There is no catch, we must start from scratch,
and we yearn for Mars, but we're stuck on Earth.

## STELLAR GRAFFITIST

Look up for the time is ripe—
not even seers would deny that.
And if stars shouldn't shoot anymore,
on account of a cosmic strike of sorts,
against man or what else I don't know—
I'd use the remains of my childhood dreams
just like fluorescent neon markers,
to streak the silence of the night with colors
and picture fireworks all across the vault.
Before I write my next piece of truth
in the shape of fluctuating lines,
my empty mug cools down,
and remembrance fails—
I'll have filled up the void I cannot name,
wiped out everlasting nothingness,
made sense of these overflowing skies,
befriended their affronting vastness.
Only then I'll be allowed to lay down the pen,
mute my conscience out awhile,
drift off to well-deserved sleep.

# ABSENCE

*There's no end to my life,*
*no beginning to my death,*
*death is life.*
—Greg Lake

Gray sky, pliable floodplain, melancholy
roads that always come full circle—enough. Voices
gone silent, glitter of whitened fields gone missing, roots
and cords once tightened gone—all is unspeakable
absence. Ubiquitous and continual,

mind-and-body-gnawing wherever I may
shelter—the murmur haunts my rebel self, winter
after winter. Like damp cold seeping into the bones.
Yet here I belong, nowhere else. Nothing can chase
me away—not what is lost, not what is left.

I'll weather the absence—whether twist of fate
or evil curse. So, I might as well keep going,
return to the ancient river's mystic shore each time
the current calls, crouch down on the big sandbar, strain
my ears to hear the rippled surface whisper,

telling me to carry on, carry on and
stain desires in paleness, muffle hopes in absence,
scavenge remembrance. Carry on like a carrion
crow—because I'll never conjure any presence
out of such a drowsy spell. And that is it,

just what I'm doing—under oath, on the road,
through secure riparian woods, over bracing
farmland, home. Till I sneak out of The Hut of Baba
Yaga, blend in by dissolving in morning mist,
finally cross The Great Gates of Kiev unseen.

# PHILOSOPHYSICS

At the end of the universe man's mind begins.
At the end of man's mind the universe begins.
Thence, there is no telling them apart—
the two often intermix, overlap, replace each other,
to the point where they can plainly be perceived as one.
They swirl around and take my head by storm
each time black coffee's pouring in the mug,
keep seething inside while a splash of milk is added,
pop in and peep out sip after sip until the final one.
When all the drink is gone—and I reemerge from it—
they're still afloat in the thin film of liquid on the bottom,
contending for space with the few grains of sugar left.

# THE FORESEEABLE COURSE OF EVENTS

It might be another asteroid,
          or maybe a comet;
it might be a spike in the solar wind,
          or a spurt of neutrinos;
it might be the eruption of all the volcanos
          found along the ring of fire.
Or it might be our inherent longing for extinction,
          as insuppressible as greediness.

        Yet we are human, and will be to the last,
        the most noxious and marvelous being
        that has ever occurred in the galaxy.
        Untamable, controversial, foolish.
        Unique, and united in one fate.
        The bizarre fate of sentience,
        and of all it has conferred
        apparent existence on.

But thirty seconds from the end, the very end of everything, when not the slightest bit of hope is left, we can still give absolute sense, more than ever, to anything, anywhere, anywhen. To reality and the multiverse itself, to our condemnation to oblivion and nihility, to our inconsequent life span. And nothing do we care about, anymore, but looking each other in the eye one last time and, as the inevitable happens, in front of eternity saying

*I love you.*

## STELLAR BOFF

Way too much of uncontrollable laughter
most of the disillusioned ones shall enjoy
at the thought of their unavailing struggle
to leave an indelible trace of their passage

fighting tooth and nail to clear some path
up to the surface of a boundless plaything
in essence consisting of structured nothing

having available just an infinitesimal of time
finally aware the whole fkn cosmic shebang
hasn't got the slightest purpose whatsoever

all while eternally rolling away in space
hopelessly stuck on a nothing of a marble
around a match flame and toward nowhere
at a speed of about nineteen miles per second.

# PAUL'S MIND

... nil ...
Out of it: all!
Us!
What!
If!
What if!

α ... ω ... α

If what?
If?
What?
Us?
Out of all: it?
... nil ...

# PRINCIPIA

Even though set in gold, a pebble remains a pebble.

Whatever reason it is said for, a lie remains a lie.

The truth is mostly found where we least look for it.

The only staple of ethics is the perpetuation of the species.

Evil does not exist per se, but as the destruction of good.

Conflict is how intelligence tries to remedy its shortcomings.

Man is not the one, is one.

Life proves reality.

Time requires life.

Reality yields time.

The universe has no end but itself.

God does make mistakes, on purpose.

## FLASH SPACERS
For the crew of the Challenger, blown up in flight on 28 January 1986

The countdown yet to end, the engines were
ignited, smoke expanded. Space dreams back
at home, secreted ones, along with fear,
last wills, unsigned, and months of notes, a stack
of abstruse papers scribbled on the sly

no one perhaps will ever find. The launch
was smooth, about a minute feeling like
the longest hour, all systems go except
the final check. No beep, no glitch, no spike.
The skyline bending quickly through the crew

compartment windows, stars appearing one
by one across the vault, the daytime night.
A few more seconds throttling up, and then
the blast: the O-rings and the cold, the flight
procedures and the windshear, all of them

had played their part. Who knows if any doubts
assailed the crew at liftoff: had they thought
the mission was secure and they would have
regained the surface safely? Sure, they sought
no fame, just heaven, still the fiercest hell

burst out of SRB's. Their shreds dispersed
among propellant spray, the boundless blue,
and ocean waves. Star sickness branded on
our wafting minds, lamenting seven who
consigned their lives to OV-99.

## STRAY TOWN

Jarring chimes. Rather groans
than clangs. The wind blowing
wild above the rooftops and no
howling through the chimneys.

Oblivion errant in the streets, the
streets entangled in the dark, the
dark abandoned in the night. The
mute ticking of haphazard clocks.

All seems to flee tomorrow, having
not recaptured yesterday. Muffled
thumping in the desert dawn. It's
not our hurried strides outbound.

It's the ground that slowly slips away
from underneath our feet. It's not us
the strangers here. It's this amnesic
town. Late in space and stray in time.

# ABANDONMENT

Soaked in silence, sunbeams through the shutters, dust
floating softly. Stuffy, flecks of mold and rust

sticking here and there, a gentle draft. The glow
makes all things appear the same as years ago,

time as if dissolved, annulled in space, and space
fixed, confined by gauds and heirlooms, still. No trace

left of sadness, grievance, anguish, though. Regret
torments just the living. Rooms are not upset,

harrowed, tortured, they can only be forlorn,
locked, concealed. Their very essence can't be torn.

Theirs is moral aging. They do not get old.

# THE MISSING WORDS

The letter never shipped. The ink
discolored, leaving subtle signs
on yellowed paper. Hard to link
to words. Entangled, cryptic lines.

Locked up, mislaid—and never found
by later dwellers—either wrong
or right, the missing words were bound
to lie forgotten far too long.

Until a child, who had been told
the story—when and where—had zest
to spare, was clever, keen and bold
enough to try, retrieved the chest.

Drawn out the sheet, she handled it
with utmost care, as if she feared
to spread some graphite over it.
As if by magic, words appeared.

# FUTURITUALISM

The third millennium really upsets our prospects,
thrusts us into futuristic worlds, where stolid robots
will do everything, from teaching kids to waging war,
from probing into space to prosecuting cybercrime,
from fixing machines to cloning brains, and more.

All people will move in self-driving, airborne cars,
planets will be terraformed by automated workforce,
parliaments and governments will be fully replaced by
AI legislators and executives, there'll be hardly need
of police and judiciary, of arrest and incarceration.

Still and all people, far too many of them, will keep
on calling for the queer, the ridiculous and the absurd,
as it really seems they can't ever do without superstition,
the mystical and the supernatural, as if such hogwash
for some odd reason were imprinted in their genes.

So, even through the fourth millennium, indeed once
we'll have encountered alien life, they'll be still revering
and resorting to these most bamboozling reference figures:
boozers, dopers, healers, mediums, quacks, soothsayers,
fortune-tellers, prophets, holy men and patron saints.

## AT THE WHITE BULL

Women, lots of women,
a whole battalion of them,
judging by their appearance
in the age range 65 to 75,
in the family restaurant
at Cannon Hall Farm.
They talk and laugh,
laugh and shout,
shout and talk all the time
across the tables put together,
seem not to bother in the least
what eats and drinks taste like.
They're having a blast, for sure.
Their inconsequential hubbies,
either at the pub or in the grave,
take good care not to complain.

## THE SWAN

Sometimes the swan believes it is a goose.
No harm done, it doesn't last long,
it almost always goes back to its old self
before taking flight.
It is when it convinces itself
it is a puissant raven—
while swimming in the pond,
afloat on such a queer assurance,
and a real raven whizzes in front of it
skimming the water—
that the problem arises.
Because then it wonders
why it cannot fly as nimbly and fast.
It often takes quite a few days
for it to repossess its identity,
but it can happen
that it never makes it again.
Eventually, evidence wipes out any doubt.
In fact, it stares at its own reflected image
ineluctably day after day
and every time it sees a swan
just below the surface
in turn looking it in the eyes
and wearing the typical fearful expression
of one that's met the ugly gaze of a raven.

# NIGHT HUNTING

The owl
on the highest branch

would swear
the moon above is

a hole
in the black curtain

over
the sun-flooded sky

made of
a billion ravens

letting
all the other birds

believe
it's time to repose

and leave
all there is to catch

to their
infallible beaks

before
he finds out the truth.

# THE URGENCY OF IMMEDIACY

Child's smile.
Innocent, uncorrupted.
Tuition, traineeship, indoctrination.
Not even a full ride on the merry-go-round
and it's already time to swell the fkn ranks,
conform, compete, produce, excel,
moil and toil to fatten up
the bloody sow.

## THE FLOOD

The river of the waiting's swelling, may overflow anyplace anytime.
It will lay waste on everything we care about, cherish the most, love.
The liars should call it quits, stop their nefarious, treacherous pep talk,
they have been pushing the envelope for too long, the measure is full.
We all, in turn, have been resting on our laurels, dazed and confused,
prey to sham and shame, dwelling on the past like immune onlookers,
pretending to be separate from the rotting, sheltered from cataclysms.
But the flood has no eyes, it's pure destructive impetus, inescapable,
nobody and nothing will stand, banks and dams will be swept away.
Once it's passed, the waiting will emerge, become novice hazarders.

# REVIVING WOUNDED KNEE

No sward, no pond, no tree is left.
Of all time the most appalling theft,
plundering, deportation, genocide.
What's become of Rain-in-the-Face,
Kicking Bear, He Dog, Spotted Elk?
What's become of their fatherland?
They'd always believed they'd win,
then hoped they'd avoid constraint,
in the end had to settle for survival.
They'd not imagined it'd be a horde,
there swarmed as many as the stars,
and brought along no happy ending.
I can't help feeling I am one of them,
*zuyá wičháša* and *wamánuŋ s'a* at once,
as my anguish trickles on both sides.
So my ghost rides about undaunted
and, though I have never been there,
leaves me entangled in one thought:
I am the prairie, and I am the bison.
I am the storm cloud on the horizon.

# ON THE RUSSIAN TRESPASS INTO UKRAINE

*It is from the hands of death people get immortality.*
—Lesya Ukrainka


Can a missile raise a stately building?
Land mines shape and tend a splendid garden?
Mortars plane and wall a handsome courtyard?
Soldiers stop a frightened child from crying?

Will one day the answers be all yesses?

Missiles keep on making buildings death traps.
Land mines keep on making gardens blood bogs.
Mortars keep on making courtyards graveyards.
Soldiers keep on making children orphans.

We abhor it all but let it happen.

# ÉMIGRÉS

No chance to fight, not even to strive,
now that the bodies twist in the slush,
and pangs are all that keep them alive.

We sold them lies, induced them to rush,
the time had come for them to just thrive,
they'd stop to creep, to run, and to crush.

They swarm the border woods like a hive,
within barbed wire, commanded to hush,
are told they're through but never arrive.

# RECURRENCE

Age of disruption.

                                                   Upheaval.

                          Derangement.

Screaming hordes at large

                                        nobody wants in the streets

                          but everybody wants to join.

Ubiquitous lies

                                          for all tastes

                          none objected to.

Just be the first

                                        to get on your soapbox

                          and sell your crap.

The fuse burns shorter

                                        while all keep blowing

                          instead of ripping it out.

Endless propaganda

                                        fed to devotees on parade

                          soon hard up without distinction.

Yes

                                        deep purple

                          ten years after.

Thunder from no stroke.

                                      Ebb from no tide.

                        One more descent into the Maelström.

## CITIZEN

I used to live in scanty clumps of tiny huts
made of earth, dung, stones, twigs and ice,
hundreds of cords away from one another,
amid boundless plains, on rivers and lakes,
at the foot of unapproachable walls of rock,
in jungles, deserts, fens, over frozen steppes.
That was believed to be the safest way to be.
Till famine or war began to visit all too often
and manhood called for gathering and unity.

I was a miner, then a mason, then a farmer
in Aleppo, cutting sandstone and gypsum,
building irrigation ditches, growing grains.
I improved all my arts and crafts in Jericho,
where I also was a shepherd and a peddler,
herding sheep and selling goods of all sorts.
I eventually became an ascetic and a soldier,
musing upon life in the temples of Varanasi
while defending its miscellaneous treasures.

So I've been spreading wealth and wonders
across the five continents and down the eras,
in Argos, Ur, Byblos, Henan, Amarna, Rome.
Today I live in huts as broad and tall as hills
obtained from forests, riverbeds, mountains.
Food, cold and perils are not issues anymore,
all I have to guard against is the air I breathe,
cute killers called PM10 and PM2.5, and bugs,
named after the letters of an eternal alphabet.

# COLLAPSE

A snip knocked down the stronghold,
a behemoth of sureties with feet of clay,
in one go, like the tiny pebble big Goliath.
Now we know we're all in the same league,
none of us leads or is able to sow new seeds.
In saecula saeculorum, as the sky implodes
over man's crazy, inconclusive endeavor,
a novel never ending flood will follow.
Who's gone, who's left, we lost count,
the background picture still unseen,
of all possible nightmares, the worst,
gulped by a bug nicknamed nineteen.
All around the globe, but America first.

# SHIMMER

Dazzled, dazed, remote ashore,
crests increase as Mistral falls.

Ancient names of winds resound,
sunken wrecks emerge and sail.

Watery pupils rove at sea,
sundown-shimmer swept away.

Boyhood days flash back to stay,
present ones run on then flee.

Pictures mingle turning pale,
some stand out and hang around:

children, sand tracks, cyclist balls,
just like forty years before.

# THE SHELL

The sea after the rain was bluer,
the beach, once dried, whiter.
I remember my first shell—
small, oddly-shaped, chipped,
a treasure, mine and no one else's,
the other children mocking me for it.
Mom had told me to clean it,
brushing and rinsing it
under running water,
to then secure it in a wooden box.
That's where it stayed for years,
till when, I really don't know.
I never lost the shell though—
I just mislaid the box.
And now, after the rain,
on the foreshore on my own,
both the sea and the beach
appear nothing more than gray.

# THE CASTAWAY

As a child he'd been feeding on sea stories, sea people, sea adventures. Benign and adverse sea, calm and rough, emerald and leaden. Tale after tale, book after book, devoured by insane desires, adrift in timeless daydream. A seagull, he'd planed over enchanted bays; sea fog, he'd enveloped mighty fleets; roller foam, he'd broken against rocks. Pirates and privateers, crossings and peripli, vanished treasures and alluring arcana, epic landings and ruinous shipwrecks filled his nights. The white whale, Sir Henry Morgan and the Maelström were his favorite talismans. Then, a boy with pristine hairs on the face, so far from the real sea, misplaced in his flatland in the middle of nowhere, he still had the sea awave inside. He could hear its call more than ever before, a wretched hero deprived of his element. Until, unaware of what lay further ahead, he saw the tempest come and crush him like a straw. Fiercer than the heaviest storm he'd ever fantasized of, truer than his rudest awakening, more untamable than his wildest dreams. Right when, alone and forlorn, he didn't have sufficient time and strength to lower the sails and take the helm.

Today he remembers with somber indifference all the hours spent on thinking, an eternally-pensive adolescent, about which album he would take to a desert island. But there is not nor ever was any such place, the tempest didn't cast him to any remote seashore. The immobile time, missed because unused, is his hermetic little world, his desert island, with no music nor sound except the howling of the wind. He thrashes around in the usual shoals, like an eel that's lost its way to Sargasso Sea but still retains a grain of hope. He keeps on clutching at the same old reef, conscious the final slip is near. He, who used to rule the seas! He fancies he is Captain Nemo at the wheel of Nautilus in the abyss once more. He sees himself a child again, when the sea fog so dear to him removes all horizons from his view.

## THE FISH

So was it the old man or the sea?
Which was Ernest's idée fixe?
His unavoidable chagrin?
His absolute eidolon?

Probably both,
maybe some hybrid,
or else neither of the two.
I'd say he never came to know.

Chasing selves against being chased.
Acting instead of playing for time.
Awareness opposed to naught.
Life at variance with death.

On the run from the lockdown,
one night under the clearest sky,
all at once the unimagined answer.
Shimmering Pisces hinted—the fish!

# TERMINAL

If you are told the time,
even though approximately,
let them know in turn.
Flat out, without remorse.
And finally speak your mind.
It'll be the most honest of you.
Or,
pretend nothing's going to happen,
don't raise the slightest suspicion.
Leave, if you find the strength.
When the time comes,
they will be grieving the least.
It'll be the most humane of you.

# PAL

He used to arrive at the last moment,
around suppertime, most of us just gone
or paying the bill, always in a hurry,
the engine running in front of the bar,
for a quick hello and a pint or two.
A young, three-girl family waited home,
the two adoring kids often planning
a surprise for him in the dining room.
He couldn't skip the appointment though,
an indispensable, long-running ritual,
a drink with the friends of a lifetime,
the ones left, mainly without a partner,
or parents, or any established routine,
heedless of domestic schedules and rules.
He rarely stayed too long, maybe never did,
disliked reneging on his promise to the crew,
but even more keeping his darlings waiting,
just delivered a joke, the anecdote of the day,
a few curt, caustic remarks on this and that.
He loved a blab about the good old times,
the lips frenziedly back and forth to the rim,
the eyes on and off his wristwatch dial.
He easily managed to empty the pint
leaving all the collar on the bottom.

A few years and his business would change.

He took to arriving quite late after dinner,
the footstep atypically slow and heavy,
a veil of sadness over the stern face,
the mind thousands of miles away,
utter disaster hanging behind the back.
A huge, corrosive, sleep-stealing burden

that would never quit him, but in the tomb.
A woodworm of guilt and victimhood.
We boozed it up until the early hours,
lost in talks on everything and nothing,
entangled in cheap, addictive pity parties.
Beer after beer, whiskey after whiskey,
although G&T was our favorite nightcap,
we often were the last regulars to go.
Memories remain, the bittersweet taste
of yesteryear, the glimpse of a smile,
the boulder of regret, a tinge of remorse.
The suspicion of having been unable
to close the circle that eats away at me.
And so nowadays, every once in a while,
late at night, when conscience too is asleep,
in the soft light of the parlor's floor lamp,
I indulge in a bit of a tipple, on my own,
whispering to myself: *Here's to you, pal.*

# THE CAR COUNTER

Standing,
    a walking stick in one hand,
        a leash in the other.
Still,
    he watches
        the rapid comings and goings
            of clouds in front of the sun.
Only,
    the collar is empty—
        Lucky was a goner years ago—
            and the dangling cord just functions
                as a second prop.
Every day
    the hours pass by quickly,
        until the shade arrives to stay.
Resolute,
    he then turns his gaze
        to the cars up and down
            the hill road in the distance,
                starts counting—
                    one every two minutes or so—
                        without batting an eyelash,
                        stops thinking.
Yet
    steady and assured—
        fatigue is not a problem—
            waiting composedly.
As if stuck
    on the pull-off of life.

## HIKER AND LINES

Mixed needles silenced your steps, so that
you hoped you could reach the tree line
undetected. Looking up, you thought
that when you were a child the conifers
didn't climb so high, while now they dared
the rock walls. Never take your eyes off
your path on a mountain slope. You
were spotted about a pitch below, stuck
among boulders by a nearly dried-up creek
encased in a secluded gully, at the foot
of an escarpment. Your true end, the
wavy snow line a couple of hours' walk
above, ruled out forever. Dusk yet far from
settling in, you hadn't realized the forest
had stopped watching over you those
last few minutes. Now you know that firs
and pines are not our guardians, but larches
are, like whose needles, at the turn of the
season, we are doomed to fall, all for
the following ones. And they who come
after trample on us, in turn, without a sound.

# THE KITE

The kite was flown
when you still had not arrived,
far with mind and body
from that unguarded edge
whereon you'd count the seconds.
It soared so plumb
that for you it was no signal
to go back on your steps,
but one final warning
not to turn around.
The sun was enlarging
above the horizon you'd been denied.
Before it got dark,
legs and arms ready for takeoff,
eyes nailed to the floor,
you launched time into space
and rose higher than upmost dreams,
beyond the first star
shyly peeping at the zenith.
No one saw you but briefly the kite.

# CATATONIA

Blade's edge awakening—dead-roar echo, deaf moan to
deceit-secreting smile—unavailingly opposes. Subdued
litany, tender liturgy—the oblation forgotten in a nook
where nobody seeks—at the day's startle on the brink of
the visible, fleetingly takes place. Blending of verity and
legend, eye not seeing what hand is gripping, finished the
sad procession, at an end the long walk—reason-doffed
and folly-decked. Herald slave to emptied thought, the
fist clenching tighter, over and over again, as if there were
no other chest, but rapture is intangible, slips like grains
of sand through the fingers—the hourglass won't collect
it. Believed of tenacious iron, silly gem gone crazy—brittle
as quickly hardened clay the dream turns out, slippery as
ice covered in a water film, more unimmobilizable than
true happiness—the one that comes unsearched for, stays
a moment and goes, right away forgotten—erelong creased
the glove that may attempt to seize it, doomed to gangrene
the delicate epidermis that may touch it. Sneaky shimmer
across the darkness, false warmth making its way, freeze
apparently driven deep in the bones—the feared memory
of the age of tears exiled on the inflection of the soul, where
the clear and the turbid ones border on each other—again
the endeavor to shake off the body jail, one last twitch of
liberation, by no-tomorrow's threshold. Flesh and spirit
neither call a truce nor continue the battle. Already the
night—portending to both the surrender to the common
enemy, permanent aphasia, absolute catatonia—peeps on
the sharp incline unfolding in front, and today—suddenly
hoary—mournfully gives itself up to history. Under the
sedimentary blankets of years, still like an old dragon—once
blaze-juggler, now unlit and buried in the moist depths of
the earth—the beveled-brimmed forge from which rare
drops of the ever bubbling yet unheard forefathers' gold

spilled out speeds up its eternal cooling. In the total absence of movement—even of dust—in the congealed becoming, in the stagnant time, in the immeasurable space, as soon as the once restless and dauntless hand wizens and stops, only the wearied lid will keep on sliding over the vitreous eye—useless vestige by then detached from the nerve. It will flap tirelessly, albeit barely, undeterred, as if seeking the vanished light, the fading glow—an ultimate remnant to attest the extinct kinesis. The scream imprisoned in the precious solidified scoria—rather, an unchanging grimace, a twisted monument to the unspoken, the unsupported, the non-strenuously defended. Neither dejection nor elation. All that might have been, should have been, and never was, didn't want to be—i   m   m   o   r   t   a   l   i   z   e   d.

## THE TRIP
After Emily Dickinson


I should have set out much sooner than I
did. By remembrances still green, winters
white, sunsets red. I cannot imagine
different colors, except for maybe blue.
The blue of dreams, blue everywhere, ever
more blue. So blue that I myself became
the blue. It resurfaces every so
often, washed-out though. Only when we're left
no choice we move, for we don't understand
we must. We're born in awe of it. The trip.


*


From colors I was flung to sounds, then to
smells and flavors, and finally to thoughts,
unaware, in the beginning, that they're
just surrogates of dreams. Ages I have
spent absorbed in thought, I haven't finished
yet. Either searching for words or trying
to word my search. I go on, not because
I need to know, but because I don't have
the slightest clue of what is coming next.
So, I might as well keep going. Going.


*

For a while the snow, as compassionate
as neglectful, covered everything and
everyone, buried fear, anxiety,
uneasiness, delusion, frustration.
They all vanished in that candor. I hoped
it would have lasted forever, like the
polar whiteout, fusing all things into
one, smoothing all asperities, making
bliss and sadness indistinguishable.
Spreading peace, so pure it seemed unreal.

\*

Then came heat, blinding light, burning of the
skin, dry mouth. And sizzling of the heart. I
always thought I would never have made it.
Yet the clanging epoch of the heroes
had begun and they, without me even
asking, for quite some time pulled my chestnuts
out of the fire, rescued me from the
quicksand of apathy, fought my uphill
battles. Till the night, the long, bitter-sweet
night suddenly led me out of the woods.

\*

All there is in the middle had better
be left alone, isn't worth bothering
about. Why dig up the past, any past,
strain memory, recall ghosts? Isn't it
the final destination that only
matters? The here and now? All the rest is
moonshine! Wipe the slate clean and start from scratch.
If it were that simple! Hardly ever
does the die roll off that way. While the past
digs up itself when we least expect it.

*

Hence came thunder and lightning, floods and droughts,
anything and everything. Everything
but the white of winters, as the green of
remembrances slowly faded too, to
pale yellow, almost transparent, and the
red of sunsets shaded off into dark
maroon, like clotted blood, and dark maroon
into black. Irreversibly. And the
blue? What's become of the once deep blue? Will
it ever recover its vividness?

*

There is who leaves, a little child, and ends
up old, having skipped the boy and the man.
There is who leaves, a little child, till he
finally reverts to a little child.
There is who leaves, a little child, and is
soon hurled into a man, then who knows what.
Lastly, there is who is born already
old, and his is an unbearably long
trip all the same. Blank, idle, misleading,
dreary. A non-trip. An insult to time.

*


And time we cannot waste on regret and
remorse. Much less on unfulfillable
wishes, these being no dreams at all. We
cannot give in to chance and randomness. Much
less to oblivion, this being the
antithesis of dreams. Whether just one
step or still a very long way to go,
whether unaccompanied or alone,
may our eyes look straight ahead, may we not
even think of turning around or back.

*

Who we have been at any stage, over
lands and under skies of any color,
along with who we could have been, they are
all but mental mirages. Siren songs,
hallucinative miasmas, snakebites.
Lethal traps. To complete the trip, we need
no one except who we are, pace after
pace, moment after moment, self after
self. And the clear vision of ourselves as
one single sequence. Ineluctable.

\*

So, I am all and none of them at once:
the baby, the child, the boy, the man, the
elder. The ghost too, for the utmost faith
in and respect for time I have. And in
the end, or nearly there, or wherever,
before my image in the mirror and
the bulk of such a giant, unseen, it
all comes down, no more and no less, to one
ancient riddle: *Was it Goliath was
too large, Or only I too small?* That's it.

## WHAT LITTLE REMAINS OF THE WINTER

The razor-thin, purple, solitary cloud has drifted away,
vanished past the undulated, pitch-black silhouette.
The upper sky is a spotless, liquid, cobalt-blue continuum,
only Venus is already visible, to the west, sharp like a pinhead,
an inch above the glowing, orange-crimson band.
Absolute silence, so dense it can be touched.
The spring, now weeks ahead, oozes through the air,
plays with lingering whiffs of chilly breeze.
Something on my mind is telling me to carry on
although the dance will soon be over.

I'm done tidying the books on the shelves
and ransacking an old shoebox for black and white pics,
many of which I didn't even imagine existed.
Some have made me laugh, others frown, still others wonder.
The hours have been passing quick, there are never enough,
all in all pleasantly, despite the dust and the backache.
I haven't found what I was looking for.
My thoughts are already running to the next winter,
the first hoarfrost, the pale sun beyond the freezing fog,
the cold, sticky, lactescent light at noon.

Notwithstanding what the calendar says
I know what the morning is bringing along instead,
and it's nothing I could use these days.
To bring my time into line I need the right sequence,
smooth and gentle, not turnarounds and rushes forward.
I'm leaving every mental eddy to the quiet of the clear night,
my raided head to the softness of the pillow,
but not before one last glance up above,
aware I can see at the most three thousand stars
among about four hundred billion more.

## THE VIXEN

She said:
*And for this—boy—you'll die.*
All froze on the instant,
then my father's friend replied:
*But you—madam—you are a vixen!*
She blurted out, irate:
*No! I'm not a vixen!*
At which he went:
*Well, then you're mad*
*like the coachman's mare!*
She stared at us
while we walked past,
I didn't speak for quite a while.

I haven't seen her since,
the hideous, sinister old woman,
and I'm still here,
some ten lusters later.
Yet, whenever I go back there,
to that secluded mountain hamlet,
and I happen to hike along
that narrow pathway
aslope among the granite chalets,
still a shiver slithers down my spine,
and I pick up my pace,
eager to leave the place,
as if I feared to spot a sign.

# THE LOSS
After Sandro Penna

The last thoughts—sunk in the pillow, hardly
turning into dreams—used to make it deep
into the night. I loved to run over the day
just passed, before moving to fancies about
the next. Always, sleep arrived too soon. The
magical aura of long summer watches—in
through the window—still is what keeps
me alive today. The child I was. But what a
child! Much of it I've brought with me so very
far away—tenacious even though unwitting.
But not everything. Time makes impetus
taper down, differences fade, both black and
white just look like gray. I no longer linger over
contemplating the evening—as if it were the
most momentous moment, the one I liked
to await after each awakening. To say it with
an honest poet's words—*My old innocence is lost.*

# THE FLICKERING

The candle flame is not for always,
its flickering is.
A child, in our old, humble flat,
I got scared to death when it went pitch dark,
all of a sudden, because of a blackout.
Quite a usual occurrence in those days.
Therefore Mom kept matches and a candle
in a specific place in every room,
although there was only one candlestick,
a cherished piece of patinated brass,
on a shelf by the kitchen window.
I miss that atmosphere,
that indefinitely lasting magic,
the quiet-voice chatting,
the Caravaggesque light
upon our faces around the table,
our gigantic shadows aquiver on the walls.
No house today holds candles,
kids don't know what blackouts are.
And yet the flickering goes on inside of me.

# WHIFFS

Light has no edge, darkness has no center, both have shape.
They visit with me briefly, quick life whiffs,
between a misty trip into nowhere and the next.
They speak a few words, terse phrases,
neat like scratches of diamond over limestone,
in a forgotten lively voice,
from a time long before they left.
I gather nothing, mostly, no real sense.
I retrieve a very distant memory, every so often,
as if arising from yesterday.
They hardly show themselves while speaking,
and when they do I can but have a fleeting glance.
Their face shines upon an invisible body,
illuminates the whole ambience,
belongs in an older past,
not the last I have known with them.
It is a face from youth,
one I am allowed to recall only when they appear.
Why do they come if they cannot stay?
How is it they take the long way around?
What do they mean?
Maybe youth is the message.
Maybe they just want me to think
I have been young, we all have, together.
There could be more I miss, I must still realize.
I may do one day, or never, but it is already enough.
A few words and a face.
A darting glow.
Whiffs.
Edge has light, center has darkness, both have no shape.

## THE HEAD OF THE FAMILY'S SENSE OF DUTY
To Dad

When you were young, toward lunchtime, Grandma
lined up half a dozen loaves of bread beside the
plate, full of boiling soup to the brim. All was
ready, neatly set on the tablecloth, perfectly on
time, so that you could start to eat as soon as you
got home and, in that one hour, also take a little
nap, before returning to the building site. Today
it takes you hours to digest a single piece of
bread, and you had to give up on your beloved
broth many a year ago. What's left of your stomach
dislikes it. And yet you still spend your life on the
site, the one within the home, twenty-four seven, like
nothing happened. There is no shortage of work, not
even while you're dreaming, or when memories, about
as old as your wedding ring, all of a sudden picture a
furtively tender smile on your shrunk but luminous face.

## ON THE SETTEE

Like he lost his tongue, he looks at her, askance,
in silence. He finds it hard to recognize
what he sees, not to mention what he hears. On
the settee, together, yet light years away,
a cruel void in between. His eyes all at
sea, at times afrown, at whom and why no one
knows, appear to say: no worries, we'll get through
this, too. But then laconic phrases, nearly
random, and queerish gestures betray the truth.
There's no return along that final stretch, not
even by a step. He spends hours in a
world no longer his, prisoner, exhausted
and half-dead inside. He cannot bring her back,
breach the barrier, break up the estranging
rigmarole. He can only sit beside her,
looking at her, askance, in silence. And wait.

## MIXED PATHOLOGY
To Mom

It's still all there,
in that slowly-shrinking pulpy mass
a little bigger than a pomegranate,
in that jumbled fistful of withering cells
no longer capable of recognizing themselves.
Every word said or heard,
every dream or thought,
every image or sound,
every emotion or feeling.
Every single moment of her life
as well as many of mine.
Everything's buried deep in there somewhere.
It must be.
Only,
the last thread left
along which all she was and is can resurface
is becoming thinner and thinner.
Until it breaks,
she prisoner inside.
Or who knows,
finally free from walls and ceilings,
unshackled from the chains
of pills and concoctions.
Yes,
free to range at will outdoors.

## AT THE SEASIDE

Her hand holds his, clenches it at times,
readily pulls his arm upward
to keep him safe from the breaking wavelets.
His little body is almost lifted off the sand.
The early-morning swash is too cold for his bare feet,
even at the height of summer.
He is a sickly child, born with a malformation,
mostly wears a shirt and a hat
even when the sky is veiled, or sunrays strike next to level.
He moans and whines, digs in his heels or wiggles around,
puts on a pouty face. Why, he doesn't really know.
Maybe he wants to be let go,
free to splash along the water's edge,
or else to collect shells and pebbles.
But Mom can see, sees well beyond the horizon.
One day, not before quite some time has forced them apart,
alone on the beach at the crack of dawn,
memories hardly emerging from the glitter,
he'll be allowed a glimpse of what alarmed her bosom's eyes.
Then all will be crystal clear:
the yanks, the rants, the harmless punishments.
He'll want to be able to go back in time,
through every single moment.
Inseparably. Hand in hand.
A child again. And everything.

## TIDES

Uncontainable tides of silence
from her telling eyes,
a whole lost world overflowing.
The sky now clear and bright,
now turbid and sullen.
Bubbling joy, unvoiced anger.
So the gestures, awkward and vague,
yet peremptory and neat, at once,
like the wind commanding the water,
now light and smiling,
now tight and anguished.
And tide after tide,
each time a new route asea,
the wind acquires the power of speech,
then shouts at my gaze,
helpless and fazed:
*I'm here, dispersed among the swells,*
*along with all my love and life,*
*adrift in myself, completely alone.*
*I've never left,*
*not even for an instant,*
*although you've heard no real sentence*
*from me for a very long time,*
*but just the broken wailing of the wind.*

# THE ABYSS

Plateaus and peaks rise for miles from the floor
but don't make it to pierce the ceiling,
their summits show through but cannot graze it.
A puny little child wearing a silly-looking straw hat,
the complexion the color of fresh milk,
Mom walking me hand in hand
along the bather-crammed waterline—
I was scared even of the smallest waves,
ran away from the uprush and the foam,
as if they could have sucked me under
and washed me offshore.
The mere idea of the abyss terrified me.
From that she always cared about protecting me.

Now that she gazes at me askance,
dark emptiness out of her pupils,
tenderly cross-eyed because of the exhausting journey
and the deepening divide,
and she hasn't had a chance to see the sea in decades—
she still tries to guard me from the abyss.
The one she's sliding into inch by inch.
Until one day eye contact and touch
will be all that's left to tie the cord.
I have long stopped to dread the billows
and learned how to come up from the depths,
but she's sunk not too far from the bottom,
while I can barely reach down to the summits.

# MICROCHIMERISM

I feel them,
the way I feel the stardust seeping through my skin.
I feel them in the light and in the dark,
in absolute silence and in deafening noise,
in peaceful days and in gloomy days,
while awake and while asleep.
They whisper to me who I am,
where I came from and where I'm headed.
They uphold me
when my body falters or my mind breaks down.
I feel them loud and clear
even though turmoil surrounds me,
and I wonder whether she can feel them in turn,
wherever she is now.
And if our swapped cells don't do the job,
I'm sure we'll join anew
as waves afloat in spacetime,
liminal ripples invisibly entwined
that eternally propagate within the whole,
within the cosmic womb astir with zillions more.

# OUR PRIVATE COSMOLOGY

I'll always mind you on that afternoon,
on day one of the strangest summer,
your spirit clutching at the oxygen mask
with every last ounce of strength.
A battered tiny body thrown aslant the bed,
the wheeze more and more accelerated,
the dilated pupils spotting my vague features
through the slits between the eyelids as heavy as lead,
just for a moment whenever I caressed your hair.
A pitiful tangle of hematomas and tubes.
Still, my mother.

And I'll always mind you there,
smiling happy on that balcony of ours,
waving at me down in the square,
when it hadn't yet been paved
and no bus line was reaching the village.
Or walking me along the shoreline
in the warmth of early morning sunshine,
shying away from the blaze and the crowds.
Or showing me the beauty of the world
from a viewpoint in the mountains,
while warning me about the cliff below.

Anguish gnaws at me,
as if I hadn't done everything I could,
but all in all I'm not afraid.
The thread is uncut,
our private cosmology remains intact,
only perspectives change.
Memories and dreams are like gravity,
they're insuppressible,
not only do they propagate in space,

but they also travel in time both ways.
So does love forever.

## MOM'S PLACE

An exact exactor, the sun broils the half-empty yard—
time and again, though not every given day—
toasts the gravel, sautés the sparse blades of grass.
Songbirds rattle off their sweet refrains—
indefatigably, every aurora through the morning—
from the poplars just outside the enclosure wall.
The unmistakable early-summer odor blend
of baked concrete and cut flowers incenses the air.
Most marble plaques run along the meridian,
on the western side, facing the crack of dawn.
Mom's five square feet lie in the first row down,
in the penumbra of the basement gallery,
where newcomers wait to don their final attire.
They're all packed and stacked—some alone,
some in twos—like on a vertical Scrabble board.
Good neighbors in the end,
nevermore intemperate or jealous,
nevermore eager to move somewhere else.
Sheltered from wind and rain, starblind, starred,
only snowflakes may pay them a call from time to time,
fluttering in through the apertures at the top of the wall.
Within time freezes, space liquefies, becoming sublimes.
And we external strangers fail to understand,
however often or seldom we betake ourselves there.

## PAREIDOLIA

So there I am again, thrown against the cirque,
to wonder what emerges frozen yonder,
wait to rebound, be finally found.
Under the mossy slate-tiled canopy,
columbines in my hand, a wish on my mind.
A torbie cat stares at me uneasy through the fence,
a ringlet flaps its wings unfrightened on my arm.
Hiding faces spy on me in sneakier ways,
from woody slopes, rocky crests, grazing clouds.
Many but the one I hoped would smile at me
and whisper *Hello, my little fawn.*
None of them knows what I went there for.
I strain to see it, eye-chew the gaping view, explore.
Alert for gales, expecting to be blown away.
I do it over, in the belief that all is set.
But it's not the time. Not now, not yet.

# LIFE

Mothers differ greatly, give existence
meaning only through their children's lifetime.
Mountains watch the snow accrue to glaciers,
till most glaciers slither back to seabeds.
Seabeds watch the storms augment the waters,
till some waters vanish into heaven.
Heaven is a place where things may happen
slowly, slowly till a secret mover
has more snow fall down to clothe the mountains.
All is plain recurrence, cycle after
cycle, which may really fool a humie's
mind, but not a mother's heart. Awareness
warrants life, while leaving mountains, seabeds,
heaven take their course. A real gift no
one requests, but all are very happy
to receive. And every single day is
like the final one, or like a new day
one, attempting to be born forever.
Children grow, pursue the light to catch a
ray of sunset through their mother's giving.

## THE INVISIBLE

I watch her watch me,
pupils into pupils,
but there's no eye contact.
Something is missing,
the intangible tie.
Souls caress for an instant
but fail to touch.
And there's no telling
what we see in each other's eyes,
if anything at all,
or just our own reflections.
A deeply buried silent cry for help,
the slowly waning shade
of the whole world we shared.
The invisible.

## ACKNOWLEDGMENTS

I am grateful to the editors of the following magazines, where nearly all the poems in this collection, sometimes in slightly different versions, have first appeared or are forthcoming:

*A New Ulster, Acumen, Dream Catcher, Focus, The Journal, Orbis, Poetry Scotland, Sentinel Literary Quarterly* in the UK;

*Adelaide, Artemis, Blue Unicorn, Blueline, The Comstock Review, Concho River Review, The Heartland Review, Inscape, Italian Americana, Light, Lit Magazine, Mizmor Anthology, North Dakota Quarterly, Nova* (formerly *Sanskrit), Pacific Review* (San Bernardino), *Pacific Review* (San Diego), *Philosophy And Literature, Poetica Magazine, Red Earth Review, San Antonio Review, San Pedro River Review, Slant, The Society Of Classical Poets' Journal, Songs Of Eretz, Spinozablue, The Stray Branch, Tipton Poetry Journal, Torrid Literature Journal, Vita Brevis Anthology, Voices In Italian Americana, The Wallace Stevens Journal, World Literature Today* in the USA;

*Cordite Poetry Review, Quadrant* in Australia;

*The Nashwaak Review* in Canada;

*The Opiate, Paris/Atlantic* in France;

*The Transnational* in Germany;

*Contemporary Literary Review India, Phenomenal Literature, Qutub Minar Review, Verbal Art* in India;

*Atelier, La Clessidra, Gradiva, Italian Poetry Review* in Italy;

*Poetry New Zealand* in New Zealand;

*New Coin, New Contrast* in South Africa;

*The Caribbean Writer* in the US Virgin Islands.

The poems *The Swan* and *The Flickering* were also included in a chapbook titled *Amalgam*, published in 2021 by Cyberwit, India.

# NOTES

In *Native Place* (p. 25), the Italian quote (from an old popular song about the village where Zanelli was born) translates as follows: *The little church there on the hill / reads the world its fate.*

*Paul's Mind* (p. 45) refers to American theoretical physicist Paul J. Steinhardt, who contributed to one of the most famous cyclic models of the universe and to laying the foundations of inflationary cosmology.

In *Flash Spacers* (p. 47), the O-rings are paired rubber seals on the joints of the solid rocket boosters for the space shuttle, supposed to prevent hot gases from escaping through the joints of the rocket's four segments; SRB stands for Solid Rocket Booster; OV-99 is the official NASA code designation for the Space Shuttle Challenger (OV stands for Orbiter Vehicle).

In *Reviving Wounded Knee* (p. 57), the Lakota expressions *zuyá wičhášá* and *wamánuŋ s'a* mean, respectively, "warrior" and "plunderer".

In *Shimmer* (p. 63), "cyclist balls" is an Italian beach game, very popular from the 1960s to the 1980s: children shape tracks on the sand and flick plastic balls along them, to imitate a cycling race. Each ball (a bit smaller than a golf ball) actually bears the picture of a famous cyclist of the time.

In the last stanza of *The Trip* (pp. 75-79), the text in italics (*Was it Goliath was too large, Or only I too small?*) is quoted from a poem by Emily Dickinson (n. 540, *I took my Power in my Hand—*).